June 20 –
1968.

With love

Robin.

The Wit of Cricket

THE WIT OF CRICKET

Compiled by

Brian Johnston

With a Foreword by

Richie Benaud, OBE

LESLIE FREWIN : LONDON

First published 1968 by
Leslie Frewin Publishers Limited,
15 Hay's Mews, Berkeley Square, London W1

This book is set in 12 on 14 point Bembo,
printed by Anchor Press and bound by
Wm Brendon, both of Tiptree, Essex

Contents

Foreword

by Richie Benaud, OBE

I AM SURPRISED anyone has had the effrontery to produce a book covering the wit of cricket : page after page of stories recording humorous moments on and off the field; anecdotes that sometimes read better than they sounded and, at other times, lose something in the telling.

I was brought up to believe there was very little that was humorous in cricket; it was a stern game played with unrelenting vigour between flannelled gods whose expression varied not, whether it be at the taking of a wicket or the smiting of some unfortunate bowler to, or over, the boundary. I was brought up not to hear barrackers, to pay no attention to various epithets they shouted from the Hill or from the Outer at the Melbourne Cricket Ground, and, in my younger days, the thought of any umpire having a sense of humour was one of the few things I found amusing in cricket.

In fact, later on I found there was much to laugh at in this great game and I have been delighted over the years to read some of the offerings in print. I am even more delighted to have the opportunity here to read the collection got together by Brian Johnston, wherein he produces some of the best anecdotes that have occurred over the years. I see he says that he has chosen his own particular favourites. This is the only way to produce a book of this kind, for not everyone's sense of humour is the same.

Some of the great characters of the game stride through this book—personalities like Walter Robins, Bomber Wells, Johnny Wardle, Freddie Trueman and the legendary WG. There is much in the book that is new and I can appreciate that there must have been quite a number of stories left out that would appeal to readers just as much as those enclosed. Much more has been written on or about cricket than about any other sport and I have been an avid reader of all sorts of cricketing books since the time I threw a tennis ball against a wall at Jugiong and developed my great love of the game.

Not all stories are obviously humorous: some have an underlying sardonic touch and others serve as great examples of human frailty, for cricket is an extremely human game. I remember in 1953 going to a marvellous country retreat some distance from London where a garden party had been arranged for the Australian side of that year. Toilet arrangements for the vast crowd were, by the standards I had known, somewhat primitive, with long queues stretching around corners and leading into small tents. A personage connected with the Australian team, and noted for his forthright speech and firm views on anything not concerned with the basic Australian way of living, had been in one of these queues for twenty minutes and was just approaching the tent flap which, by this stage, looked to him something like Valhalla.

At that moment a well-known peer of the realm wandered past the queue and, lost in thought, started to push his way into the tent. He was arrested by a firm hand on the shoulder and a broad grating Australian accent: 'Eh, mug, where the 'ell do you think you're going? Get back in the queue like the rest of us.' Very human! So like the game of cricket itself—triumph for one and disaster for the other.

I visited England in 1953, 1956 and 1961 as a player and have travelled on a number of occasions to cover various Test series in that country. There has been a lot of talk in recent years that the characters are going from the game, and I think possibly this is true; that a different type of cricket is played now, one that is supposed to conform to an expected pattern rather than produce any individual personality. Cricketers like Freddie Trueman will always be characters simply because they are of strong personality and will resist any attempts to subjugate them to the ordinary. But it is not easy for young players in any country these days to be characters, even in private, let alone public.

I like the story in this book where Trueman is quoted as being in competition with Wes Hall, and of the modern-day players there would appear to be more stories—some of them apocryphal—concerning Trueman than of any other player. Freddie lends himself to stories, and I suspect that some of those I have credited him with over the years at cricket dinner functions might well have belonged to someone else.

But they sound like Freddie as I have known him—one of the great characters over the years—and, as the audience accepts this as a known fact, he gets the credit. There was the occasion when Freddie was playing in a match in Yorkshire against a team captained by a bristling moustached ex-Major, replete with silk cravat and gaudily striped cap. Freddie had been unfortunately dismissed first ball, with the Major urging the opposing bowler 'to attack this man Trueman'. And then, when the Major came in stuffily demanding one to get off the mark, Freddie acquiesced with the postscript: 'And with t'next ball, I'll pin you to bloody sightscreen.' Perhaps it was Freddie, perhaps it was someone else, but I like it and, for me, it is part of the wit of cricket.

I heard Humphrey Tilling's story concerning the Four Ages and was captivated by it at the time. Public speaking is a great art and he is one of the greats in this particular field which has produced some remarkably fine stories over the many years of the game. To listen to Sir Norman Birkett when he made his famous remark to Ian Craig in 1953 and to hear modern-day cricket humorists like John Warr in action is a great privilege. So too is it a privilege to read humour from those like Ian Peebles who tells the marvellous story about Alf Gover on page 65.

My own favourite is another of Peebles' offerings wherein he tells the story of the village parson who had played for twenty years in the village cricket team but only with indifferent success, scoring forty runs and taking six wickets in this time and never managing to hold a catch. On the great day when the neighbouring village provided the opposition the vicar, moving nimbly to his right at long-on, took an astonishing one-handed catch to the plaudits of a considerable crowd present. Tossing the ball up and catching it again as the crowd continued to shout, he eventually lay down on the lush outfield, rolled the ball down his nose, past his chin and bounced it up and down on his now considerably expanded chest. Whereupon mid-on arrived breathless and shouted at him : 'Throw it in you old fool, it was a no ball and they've run seven.'

Ah well, things like this happening on the village green are as much part and parcel of the game as the humour associated with the great players. I am delighted Brian Johnston, himself a man of not inconsiderable wit, has seen fit to chronicle some of the things that over the years have added spice to a great game.

Introduction

WIT IS DEFINED in the Oxford Dictionary as 'that quality of speech or writing which consists in the apt association of thought and expression calculated to surprise and to delight by its unexpectedness – the utterance of brilliant or sparkling things in an amusing way'. To this I would add the skill, perception and humour of the cartoonist.

This book is not just another collection of humorous cricket stories. Instead, I have tried to collect a number of witty sayings, writings and cartoons by people about cricket. More witty remarks are quoted, more books or articles are written, and more speeches made, about cricket than about all other games put together. The more leisurely and friendly tempo of the game lends itself to the witty exchange between players – something for which there never seems time on the football field. I make no claim to the originality of any of the contents. Many of them have been passed around and around among cricketers of all ages and times. Most of them I hope are true, though some may have been embellished in the telling. But I have deliberately eschewed anything known to be fiction – that has been well covered in several other books.

I am most grateful to everyone whose remark or piece of

writing is included in these pages. Without them there would have been no book! Finally, I am well aware that there is much wit for which I have not had room. But I have chosen my own particular favourites, and only hope that they will give you as much pleasure and laughter as they have given me.

BRIAN JOHNSTON

Barrackers

One hears a great deal about the wit of the barracker, especially from the Hill at Sydney where the famous Yabba, with his loud voice, used to flay friend and foe alike with his barbed wit. But in cold print most of the barracking seems rather tame and flat. Like most spontaneous remarks it does not easily bear repetition. However, here are a few samples of the sort of thing which at the time gets roars of laughter from the crowd on the ground.

Wes Hall was bowling to 'Slasher' Mackay during the West Indies Tour of Australia in 1960–61. Slasher was playing a dead bat at every ball. A wag in the crowd called out:

Hey, Mackay – you'll never die of a stroke!

* * *

At Brisbane in 1954 Trevor Bailey came on to bowl ten minutes before close of play. England had been in the field all day and

Australia had scored 208 for two. Bailey, as usual, put down the ball, paced out his run, and then took a trial run to check up on his action – without, of course, the ball. From the crowd, a loud voice, obviously encouraged by a fair consumption of beer during the day, called out:

And that's your best bloody ball Terdyee Bylee.

* * *

During the MCC Tour of Australia in 1965–66 Bill Lawry made a succession of large scores in the Tests but always took a mighty long time over it. On one occasion an Australian barracker could stand it no longer:

What's the matter, Lawry? Have you taken the Pill?

* * *

Inebriated barracker on the Hill to the late Nawab of Pataudi during the MCC 1932–33 tour:

Say, Gandhi, where's your goat?

PATAUDI: I don't know but, from the smell, I should say you have it with you!

* * *

During Len Hutton's tour of Australia, Frank Tyson's tremendous speed caused dismay and destruction amongst batsmen wherever he bowled. On one occasion when he was at his fastest, he had run through a side until it was the turn of the number eleven batsman to come in. Looking pale and apprehensive he came down the pavilion steps, but was so nervous that he couldn't close the catch of the pavilion gate. A voice from the crowd shouted:

Leave it open, you won't be long!

* * *

A batsman had played and missed a number of times. Yabba, the famous Sydney Hill barracker, shouted out to the bowler:

Send him down a grand piano, and see if he can play *that*!

* * *

Once on the 1920–21 tour of Australia J W (Young Jack) Hearne had been batting for a very long time without scoring a run. Suddenly he tapped the ball on the off-side and scampered down the pitch for a short single. Shouted Yabba:

Whoa! He's bolted.

* * *

Ray Robinson tells of the occasion when umpire George Borwick was signalling to an attendant who was moving the sightscreen at the batsman's request. Borwick was holding his arm aloft for quite a long time as a signal to the attendant to keep on pushing. Yabba noticed the upstretched arm and shouted:

It's no use, umpire – you'll have to wait till the lunch interval, like the rest of us!

It's all right for you, 'keeper – you've got gloves to protect you from all the sweat and spittle they're putting on the ball.

Cricket Dinners

CRICKET DINNERS ARE as much a part of cricket as the game which goes on out in the middle. They are an annual ritual for almost every cricket club in the land, and although the food and drink are important, it is the standard of speeches by which the success of a dinner is usually judged.

John Warr on the difficult art of after-dinner speeches at cricket dinners:

The Chinese may have invented gunpowder, the Americans may have thought of cut bread, and the Russians certainly produced the first iron curtain, but nobody can deny that we in this country devised the ritual of the club dinner.

Such functions do not run in seasons, but grind on remorselessly through the whole year with the coffee cups of one thrash cleared in time to make way for the soup plates of another. Our whole roast chicken industry depends on the annual get-together of countless societies and associations.

Usually held on Friday or Saturday to allow a vital recovery period the following day, only the flimsiest excuse is necessary for the wine glasses to be raised and the speech-making to start.

Certainly in cricket there is no shortage of such functions and each has the built-in pitfalls that the wine glasses may be raised too often and that the speech-making may last too long.

On one famous occasion I well remember making polite conversation to a club president when I heard a dull splash on my left. Unaccustomed to pre-dinner drinking his wife had fainted face-down in the tomato soup.

Fortunately mass catering came to her rescue, because the soup was too cold to burn and not deep enough for drowning. She staged a gallant recovery in time for the cheese and biscuits.

At another function a local tycoon invited a number of guests back to his house after the dinner. Unfortunately, as a vice-president, a past captain and a life member of more than forty years standing etc, he had fitted into every category for the purpose of taking wine.

At the close of the dinner he was practically flat out and he must go on record as the only host to be carried into his own party.

For every man who succumbs to alcohol there are five others who have been brain-washed and paralysed by the speech-makers. Some strange mania seems to seize a man called upon to address his friends in public. One chairman took fifteen minutes to propose the loyal toast which properly done should consist of two words.

I still wince when I recall a dinner where there were twelve speeches and two professional entertainers. The last orator rose at ten minutes past midnight and he spoke for twenty-three minutes. His audience had thinned out to three people by the end and two of them were his brothers.

One distinguished cricket correspondent once spoke for so long that the audience were not tapping their watches as much as looking at the calendar.

On rare occasions the twin snags of excessive wine plus a speech to go with it are woven inextricably together. Such a moment occurred when a distinguished Welsh sportsman, perhaps more famous for his rugby football prowess than his skill at cricket, was invited to attend the Mumbles Cricket Club dinner.

To give you an idea of the travelling involved, Swansea is regarded by the locals as a suburb of Mumbles and the round trip from London is some 430 miles. On arrival on Friday evening my colleague enjoyed some typical Welsh hospitality at the charming home of a local solicitor. The drinks were roughly ninety-nine parts gin to one part tonic.

At all events we moved off uncertainly to the meal held at a local hotel. As my friend was making the main speech of the evening and further refreshment was circulating freely I kept a close eye on his condition. He was seated in front of a hot radiator, and the various drinks inside him were curdling and fermenting nicely.

At 10 pm the chairman rapped the table and called upon our friend to propose the toast of cricket. He rose to his feet, his lips twitched, but no sound emerged. It was at this point that he offered the greatest compliment that has ever been paid to a single cricketer. For through the mists of alcohol one single vision must have emerged, perhaps a cover drive perfectly executed.

'Wally Hammond was a jolly good player,' came the words erratically delivered but none-the-less sincere, and then came the slow but definite collapse of the speaker.

Whichever way you look at it, it works out at over sixty miles a word.

* * *

A gentleman called Low about a fellow guest called Rickett:

If letter C were to your name before,
Much as we like you friend, we all should like you more.

To which in his *speech Rickett replied:*

If before your name were placed the letter S,
Much as we cricketers like you now, we should like you less.

* * *

Unfortunately most speeches are made from notes and only a few have been recorded on paper. In general they lose a great deal in the process and make unsatisfactory reading. However, one of the most brilliant, which has probably become the most famous of all, was recorded on tape. It was by Humphrey Tilling at the Silver Jubilee Dinner of the Forty Club in 1961, and must be one of the few after-dinner speeches on any subject to be greeted by a standing ovation. Inevitably a certain amount is lost by not hearing his fine speaking voice and remarkable timing:

Gentlemen. It occurred to me that although there are not seven ages of cricket, there are at least four, and I thought it might be salutary for us all, if I gave you a short description of each of these ages, if you would honestly try when I have finished to place yourself in the age in which you think you should be placed.

The first age I call the age of Innocence or Youth. The age when you arrive at the cricket ground half an hour before the match is supposed to start. The age when it is only a question of whether you bat number one or number two; where it's a question, as far as bowling is concerned, at which end you open; where you walk as of right to cover point; where your definition of a quick run is a fairly thick edge to first slip; when to wear a box is a sign of extreme effeminacy; and when after the game you jump into some fast sports car, in the passenger seat of which is seated a delicious blonde, you drive away happy with the thought that she will be easier to attain than that century which the scorer was at that moment inscribing in the book against your name.

The second age is the age of Discretion. The age of Maturity. This is the age when you arrive on the ground just as the umpires are walking out. The age when, with difficulty, you can be persuaded to bat as high as number six; when you accept and sometimes get a couple of overs before tea when the match is over. The age when to forget your box is worse than forgetting your wife's birthday; the age when after the game you slip off quickly home in the car to your wife to avoid a row.

And the third age is the age of Senility. This is the age when to be placed number ten is just a little too high; where to be asked to bowl is a deliberate and calculated insult. The age when fielding is only possible with the feet. The age when you define a short run as a very slow hit ball to deep extra-cover. The age when your box has become a permanent appendage to your truss. The age when after the game you may be found sitting in the local pub, harbouring improper and alas, impractical thoughts about the aged and unattractive barmaid.

And the fourth age, the age of Retirement; when no longer can you play. When you perambulate around the perimeter of the ground – a magnificent silhouette against the dying sun. When you pour out to anyone foolish enough to listen an unending stream of apocryphal stories of your youth. The age when your box reposes on your dressing-table, a receptacle for spare collar studs. The age, alas, when sex is no more than a Latin numeral.

* * *

The late Lord Birkett was perhaps the most sought-after speaker for any great cricket occasion. His presence and beautiful voice lent quality to his material which was always witty and expressive proof of his great affection for cricket. In 1953 he proposed the health of the Australian cricket team at the Cricket Writers' Dinner in the Skinners' Hall. He had this to say of the baby of the team – Ian Craig, then aged only seventeen:

. . . Every mother in England will pray for him – at his going in and his coming out.

* * *

The late Sir Noel Curtis-Bennett, who did such wonderful work for boys' clubs, told how he was once visiting a club in the back streets of London:

A game of cricket was going on in the street and I noticed one small boy sitting on the ground crying. I went and lifted him up to try and console him. One of the other small boys immediately piped up 'Hi guv, what yer doing wiv 'im? Put 'im dahn – e's our wicket!'

*   *   *

Sir James Barrie at a dinner given by the Authors' Club for Sir Pelham Warner – before he was knighted:

On the first occasion I saw Mr Warner bat he made – er – one. On the second occasion I regret to say he was – humph – not *quite* so successful.

Ninety-two for four.

Players

THERE IS NO doubt that much witty repartee takes place between players both on the field and in the pavilion, but because of its spontaneity and the fact that it is frequently unheard by others, much of it goes unrecorded. Here are a few instances that have survived:

Surrey were playing an away match at a seaside resort and, during one of the intervals, Alec Bedser was followed by a long line of children eager to get his autograph. When he reached the Pavilion steps he turned round and said good-naturedly to them:

Who do you think *I* am? – the Pied Piper of Hambledon?

* * *

John Bradman (son of Sir Donald), on returning from school one day after playing cricket in a home match:

SIR DON: Well, how did you get on?

JOHN: All right, Dad, but they have a funny rule at school. If a fellow scores fifty he has to retire. But I tricked them! When I reached forty-nine I hit a four.

* * *

Ian Craig aged seventeen, was addressed by the Queen at Lord's when the Australians were playing Middlesex in 1953:

THE QUEEN: I understand this is your first visit to England, Mr Craig.
CRAIG: Yes, Your Majesty, and unless my batting improves it will also be my last!

* * *

On one occasion in the 'thirties a raw young amateur was captaining Leicestershire when E W Dawson was unable to play, as in those days it was more or less unheard of for the senior professional to be allowed to captain the side. The opposition batted and had made well over three hundred by six o'clock with very few wickets down. Not once had the young amateur consulted George Geary about the bowling changes. At last in desperation he did go up to him and asked George who he thought should be put on:

Put the clock on, and then we can all go home.

* * *

Dr W G Grace had just packed his bag one morning and was ready to go off to play for Gloucestershire, when a lady rushed up to his door and said: 'Can you come quickly, Doctor, I think my twins have got the measles':

I'm sorry, Ma'am, but I am just going off to Gloucester to play cricket and can't stop. But contact me at the ground if their temperatures reach 210 for two.

* * *

After suffering from a surfeit of dropped catches in the slips off his bowling, Alf Gover, was having a drink with some of the offenders after close of play. After a while one of them said: 'Well, so long Alf, I must be off. I've got a train to catch.' Alf replied:

So long. Hope you have better luck – with the train!

* * *

At Cheltenham when Surrey were playing Gloucestershire Gover was asked by umpire Bill Reeves whether he wanted guard:

No, thanks, I've played here before.

* * *

At the Scarborough Festival on one occasion Freddie Trueman came in to bat against Wes Hall. Freddie snicked his first four balls through the slips, at which Wes Hall stamped down the pitch and said to him:

Where did you learn *your* cricket? EDGEbaston?

* * *

Brian Statham, about a certain Test bowler who was known to be a chucker:

He ought to get a job as professional at HURLingham.

* * *

Patsy Hendren was fond of telling this apocryphal (I hope!) story. Once when travelling in a train on his way to a match he sat opposite an ashen-faced stranger, who had his coat collar turned up around his ears. He looked so ill and thoroughly miserable that Patsy was moved to ask him what the trouble was. In a hoarse whisper – hardly able to speak – the man confided that he was a very keen cricketer, but had recently let his side down badly by making five ducks in a row. Said Patsy:

Oh dear, oh dear, if I ever made five ducks in a row I would cut my throat.

The Stranger (in a whisper): I have.

* * *

Hendren to a barracker, after he had missed a sitter on the boundary, and the barracker had shouted: 'You ought to get a good big sack':

If I'd a sack as big as your mouth . . .

* * *

Once in Australia, a very high catch was hit to Hendren in the deep field. As the ball soared higher and higher into the air, a voice from the crowd shouted: 'Drop it, drop it and I'll let you kiss my sister.' Someone, in later years, asked Patsy what he had done:

As I hadn't seen his sister, I caught the ball.

* * *

Eric Hollies to a barracker in Australia who had asked sarcastically, 'Do they still bury their dead in Birmingham?':

No. They stuff them and send 'em out here.

* * *

Len Hutton – on lady cricketers:

Ladies playing cricket – absurd. Just like a man trying to knit.

* * *

When Colin Ingleby-Mackenzie was captain of Jim Swanton's XI in Trinidad in 1961, Jim was worried by the many late nights which the team were keeping, resulting in a loss of form. He summoned a meeting and suggested that in future the team all got to bed by eleven o'clock. He then, perhaps unwisely, asked Colin, the captain, to comment:

I don't see how we can be in bed at eleven, when we have to be out on the field at half-past!

* * *

Roy Kilner about one of his tougher Yorkshire colleagues:

If he had taken all ten wickets in an innings, he would have grudged the chap who was not out.

* * *

C J Kortwright to W G Grace after the Doctor had failed to go when given not out on two consecutive balls – one palpably LBW, the other a loud click into the wicketkeeper's gloves. With the third ball Kortwright knocked back the middle and leg stumps:

Surely you're not going, Doctor? There's one stump still standing!

* * *

On a sweltering day at Edgbaston George Gunn and 'Dodger' Whysall opened for Notts – George wearing a white panama hat. He scored twenty in fifteen minutes, then tamely returned a half volley to the bowler. His captain Arthur Carr said to him in the dressing room: 'Good heavens, George, what were you doing to get out to a ball like that?':

Too hot, sir.

* * *

Maurice Leyland to Len Hutton who, aged seventeen, was run out for nought in his first match for Yorkshire:

Never mind, Leonard – tha's started at t'bottom.

*   *   *

Leyland to Johnny Wardle:

WARDLE: You know every time I bowl a bad ball I could kick myself.
LEYLAND: Could you now? Nay, Johnny, tha' must be black and blue.

*   *   *

On the famous occasion when Victoria scored 1,107 against New South Wales for whom Arthur Mailey was bowling; his figures were four for 362. He said afterwards:

I should have had an even better analysis if a bloke in a brown trilby hat sitting in the sixth row of the Pavilion roof hadn't dropped two sitters!

*   *   *

Cecil Parkin, about a fellow member of the MCC team to Australia in 1920–21 after a rough journey through the Bay of Biscay:

We were all seasick except———. He was too blooming mean to part with anything!

* * *

And to his captain, Johnny Douglas, whose bowling figures were nought for plenty on the board, yet still kept himself on, Parkin suggested:

Why not go on at t'other end: maybe tha'll see score board better from there.

* * *

In 1921 H L (Horseshoe) Collins batted five and a half hours for forty runs in the Fourth Test at Old Trafford. One of the exasperated spectators finally shouted out to the England captain, Lionel Tennyson:

Why don't you recite to him one of your grandfather's poems?

THE IMPERIAL CRICKET CONFERENCE
at Lord's
All those in favour of CHUCKING?
Roy ULLYETT.

To which Parkin is said to have shouted back:

He has done, that's why Collins has gone to sleep!

* * *

Percy Perrin, on being asked whether he had saved the boundary after one big hit into the deep field:

Yes, I certainly did – but mind you, they ran eight.

* * *

Fred Price once caught seven catches in an innings when keeping wicket for Middlesex against Yorkshire at Lord's. When he was having a drink in the Tavern afterwards a lady came up to him and said: 'Oh, Mr Price, I did *admire your wicketkeeping today. I was so excited I nearly fell off the balcony.':*

If you had done so madam, on today's form I would have probably caught you, too.

* * *

Wilfred Rhodes was bowling in the nets to a boy at Harrow whose eye was better than his technique. He never got his left foot across, but even so kept hitting the ball a long way out of the net. After one particularly big hit Wilfred called out: 'Look at your feet. Look at your feet.':

The pupil replied: Never mind my feet, you look at the bloody ball.

* * *

Yorkshire were playing Somerset in the good old days. Emmott Robinson was bowling when in came the next batsman; a real gentleman, Zingari bristling moustache, silk shirt ('Never wore a vest in my life!'), spotless batting trousers, well whitened pads and boots, and a highly coloured fancy cap. 'Good morning, Robinson,' he said on his way to the wicket. Emmott took an immediate dislike to him. The batsman arrived at the wicket, took guard, and then spent ages looking round the field, strutting around as he did so. At last the batsman was ready, and Emmott bowled him a snorter, pitching on the leg stump and hitting the top of the off. On his way out the batsman said:

Well bowled, Robinson, it was a fine ball.

Emmott replied:

Aye, but t'were wasted on thee.

*　　*　　*

E J (Tiger) Smith:

I never missed a catch in my life. They just dropped out!

*　　*　　*

Said by Joe Hardstaff of Roly Thompson of Warwickshire who used to take an unnecessarily long run:

He takes such a long run that you're out of form by the time he reaches the stumps.

*　　*　　*

R T Stanyforth, the wicketkeeper, who captained MCC in South Africa in 1927–28, had not a great reputation as a batsman. On one occasion on the tour he rose to make an after-dinner speech, knocking over his chair which fell with a clatter on the floor behind him. Quite unmoved he said:

It's all right, Gentlemen, I'm used to the sound of falling timber behind me!

* * *

Bertie Oldfield had twice been given not out LBW in one over and on both occasions Maurice Tate obviously thought he was out. At the end of the over he walked menacingly up to Oldfield and from behind his usual cupped hand said:

'Ot, ain't it?

* * *

C J 'Buns' Thornton was one of the biggest hitters the game has ever known, and his favourite hunting ground was Scarborough during the Festival. On one occasion he was in tremendous form and hit two sixes off successive balls, both of which broke the same window of a house overlooking the ground. Somewhat naturally the owner protested. Thornton said apologetically:

Well, perhaps you ought to leave it open. . . .

* * *

In the Fifth Test at the Oval in 1938 Arthur Wood came in to bat at number eight when the score was 770 for six. When he returned to the pavilion after a hard-hit fifty-three, he and Joe Hardstaff had put on another 106 runs and the score stood at 876 for seven. As Arthur made his way back up the pavilion steps he turned to a member and said:

Just like me to get out in a crisis!

* * *

Johnny Wardle, playing in a local league match when coaching in South Africa, was hit by the batsman three times to cover-point, and each time the fieldsman there let it go between his legs for four. Johnny asked the captain:

Couldn't we ask the gentleman to put his legs together?

Oh no. We mustn't offend him. He's the local Scoutmaster.

Then send for Baden-Powell. At least that will make him stand to attention!

* * *

Facing Ray Lindwall for the first time, Johnny Wardle's bat was shaking in his hands as he took guard. 'Now come on. What do you want?' said umpire Frank Chester impatiently:

A slow full toss down the leg side, please.

* * *

In Australia in 1950–51 J J Warr had the following bowling analysis – 73–6–281–1. Someone, not believing these figures, queried the number of runs. 'No,' said John, 'they are right. I remember the figure exactly. Hymns Ancient and Modern No 281':

Art thou weary, art thou languid, art thou sore distressed?

* * *

Middlesex once had to follow on after some very bad batting. One of the Middlesex batsmen in the dressing-room called out: 'What's the order in the second innings, skipper?' To which John Warr replied:

Same order – Different batting.

* * *

When 'Bomber' Wells came in to bat for Nottinghamshire against the Australians at Trent Bridge in 1964, Neil Hawke was in devastating form. The umpire, ready to give him guard, said: 'What do you want, Bomber?':

Help!

* * *

Arthur Wood, to a batsman who had played and missed at three successive balls, each of which just grazed the stumps without disturbing the bails:

Have you ever tried walking on water?

* * *

And to Hedley Verity at Bramall Lane in 1935, after H B Cameron had just hit Verity for thirty in one over Wood offered this advice:

Keep 'em there Hedley. Thou hast him in two minds – he don't know whether t'smack thee for four or six.

* * *

Frank Woolley to A J Evans after a succession of dropped catches by G B Legge, A J Evans and himself:

You know, sir, about the epidemic, don't you? – the one that's not catching.

* * *

On one MCC tour a well-known England cricketer was being taken round an eastern potentate's harem. After admiring the dusky beauties lying around all over the place he asked his host how many of them he had altogether:

At the last count 198.
A pity; two more and you could have a new ball.

* * *

In the days when that great character, Gerry Weigall, was Captain of the Kent Second Eleven, they were playing an away match on a ground which perhaps should remain nameless. The pitch looked terrible and was difficult to distinguish from the surrounding field. Gerry Weigall won the toss and took his senior professional, George Fenner, out to look at the pitch:

What do you think I ought to do, George, bat or put them in?

If I were you, sir, I should bat before the flowers start coming up!

*   *   *

Derief Taylor of Warwickshire was once given out LBW after being hit on the batting glove by the ball. After a moment of stupefaction he turned and ran back all the way to the pavilion:

UMPIRE: What's the matter? Why has he run off like that?

One of the fielders: He's gone to get a knife!

Umpires

THE RELATIONSHIP between cricketers and umpires is on a much more friendly basis than that between footballers and referees. In the winter game the referee is so obviously an official. The same dark shorts, the shirt cuffs turned up at the sleeve, the boots with laces tied under the instep and so on – all these tend to make him an impersonal adjudicator of the laws. He also has a further sign of authority – the whistle. This not only confirms his official status but, without meaning to, often appears to make him sound officious.

But in cricket it is all so much more casual and friendly. One umpire may wear a trilby hat, another a cloth cap. Some wear brown boots, others white. This all helps to create a less formal atmosphere. And a most important thing – there is no little black book in which to take cricketers' names! And so it is inevitable that there are countless examples of wit exchanged between player and umpire and *vice-versa*. On the whole, the umpire usually seems to come off best.

R A Fitzgerald, Secretary of MCC (1863–76), once gave the following definition of what he considered an umpire should *be:*

. . . An umpire *should* be a man – they are, for the most part, old women – and he *should* have had a thorough practical initiation into the mysteries of the game. It is not necessary for him to be able to repeat the laws of cricket by heart, though it wouldn't materially injure him if he could, but he *should* be ready at all times to give a prompt and decisive answer on questions of practical import at issue during the game. He *should* not only keep his eyes open, but keep them fixed on the game; he *should* be able to count correctly, at least up to 'four', if not to 'six', and to apply this scanty gleaning of arithmetic to the given quantity of balls per over. He *should* be the first to appear at the wickets, and the last to leave them, he *should* avoid conversation with the field, *should* be above all suspicion of bias, and free from all odour of the tavern. A foreigner might fancy it were needless (but it is *not* by any means) to say that at all times his manner *should* be courteous and respectful, and that his decision, though given promptly, *should* invariably be served up without sauce or seasoning of his own. An umpire *should* consider himself a chronometer set for the day, regulated according to the intervals allotted to play and refreshment. He *should* be careful to see that time is not unnecessarily wasted, and if he cannot at all times command attention, *should* not therefore be the less ready to call 'Play'.

* * *

Alec Skelding's regular comment as he removed the bails at the close of play:

And that, gentlemen, concludes the entertainment for the day.

* * *

Skelding after an appeal for a run-out which was a very close thing:

Gentlemen – it's a photo finish – and I haven't got time to develop the photo. NOT OUT.

* * *

Charlie Knott of Hampshire was bowling to Dusty Rhodes of Derbyshire and roared out a terrific appeal for a catch at the wicket. 'Howizeee?'

ALEC SKELDING: Oh, he's not at all well and was even worse last night.

* * *

Alec Skelding was umpiring a match on a hot, dusty day. One of the bowlers had a full set of false teeth, and as he ran up to deliver a particularly fast ball all his teeth fell out on to the ground. The ball hit the batsman on the pad and the bowler turned round and mouthed unintelligible noises. Alec, quick to see what had happened, said 'I beg your pardon. I cannot tell what you say.' The bowler tried again but Alec still pretended he could not distinguish his words. So the bowler stooped down, recovered his dentures covered in dust, replaced them and turning round said rather grittily:

How's that?
Not out!

* * *

An umpire (who shall be nameless) after Johnny Wardle enquired: 'You know, I think that ball would have hit the wicket. Where do you think it would have hit?':

How should I know – the gentleman's leg was in the way!

* * *

A bowler kept on knocking into a very fat umpire during his run up to the wicket. He asked him if he would mind standing sideways

I will, but I warn you, it's worse!

* * *

Attributed to several umpires:

Very slow bowler: How's that?
Umpire: Not out.
Very slow bowler: It pitched straight didn't it.
Umpire: Yes.
Very slow bowler: It didn't turn, did it?
Umpire: No.
Very slow bowler: He didn't touch it, did he?
Umpire: No.
Very slow bowler: Then, why wasn't he out?
Umpire: It wasn't going fast enough to distu rb the bails

* * *

Bill Reeves once gave a batsman not out LBW in reply to a loud appeal from George Macaulay, and a few balls later again said no to a similar appeal:

GEORGE: What was the matter *that* time?
REEVES: Too high.

In the next over bowled by Macaulay there was an even more confident appeal for LBW and again Reeves gave it not out:

GEORGE: What was wrong *this* time?
REEVES (quite unmoved): Too low.

* * *

In a Middlesex match before the war R W V Robins had just completed a very expensive over and decided it was time to make a change. He called over to Jim Smith, the giant Middlesex fast bowler: 'Take the next over at this end, Jim.' Hearing him, Reeves walked up to Robins who wasn't in a very good temper:

Do you want your sweater, sir?

It was a very hot day and Robins replied grumpily:

You can keep the bloody sweater and you know what you can do with it.

What, sir? Swords and all?

* * *

When he was at school the late Gilbert Harding hated cricket. The headmaster, appreciating this, excused him playing on condition that he took some exercise such as walking or tennis. But the games master was always very annoyed about this and got his own back one day (so he thought) by making Gilbert Harding umpire in the annual match of the masters v the boys. The masters batted first and the games master, resplendent in his Oxford Authentic cap, batted superbly and was ninety-nine not out when a bowler from the end at which Gilbert Harding was umpiring hit him high up on the left thigh. 'How's that?' said the bowler.:

Out.

The games master was furious and, as he passed Gilbert on his way back to the pavilion, said: 'Harding, you weren't paying attention. I wasn't out.':

GILBERT: On the contrary, I WAS paying attention and you weren't out.

*   *   *

A ball bowled by Ray Smith of Essex struck the batsman on the pads, and Ray inquired innocently of Frank Lee, 'Was that close?':

Yes, it was close.
Ray insisted: Very close?
Yes, very close.

With that Ray let out a yell:

How was it then?
Not close *enough.*

* * *

In an up-country match in Australia Godfrey Evans brought off a magnificent leg-side stumping. As he whipped off the bails he shouted to the umpire: 'How's that?':

Bloody marvellous.

* * *

The captain of the village side to a man called in to umpire at the last moment, who admitted that he knew nothing of the laws of cricket:

We're fielding first and all that you have to do is, when anybody says 'How's that', just say 'Out'. Later on when we go in to bat, I'll tell you a little more!

* * *

W G Grace was batting on a very windy day and a fast bowler bowled a ball which just flicked off the bails. The Doctor stood his ground, calling out to the umpire: 'Windy day today, Umpire.':

Yes, very windy indeed, and mind it doesn't blow your cap off on the way back to the pavilion.

*   *   *

When he was a young man Frank Tyson went into bat against a team of first-class cricketers. His form was not very good. He missed the first ball, the next hit him on the pad, he snicked the third and was clean bowled by the fourth. As he walked off the umpire said to him:

Aye lad, tha was lucky to make nought.

*   *   *

Albert Gaskell, the first-class umpire, is very broad and weighs over eighteen stone. He says that his wife sometimes goes to watch a game when he is umpiring and tells him she can easily recognise him because:

If it moves it's you, if it doesn't, it's the sightscreen!

Writing in 'Punch', *Bernard Hollowood once suggested the following ploy on appealing to umpires:*

Try a sudden ' 'owzat?' or 'How would that be?' (according to umpire) at odd moments during the game – preferably while the ball is motionless. There are umpires who react favourably, anxious to prove their knowledge of the game's finer points and perhaps their wakefulness.

A week or so ago I appealed violently from cover point while a sightscreen was being moved. The umpire shot a quick look at me: 'I see what you're after,' he said, 'you're just a little too previous.' I let him see that I was disappointed.

Four balls later, while the batsmen were running a sharp single, I appealed again. There was no mistake this time. As the outgoing batsman was out-going I strolled over to the umpire and congratulated him on his powers of perception.

'You're a sharp 'un, sir, you are,' he said, 'an' no mistake.'

See what I mean?

Watching Cricket

MOST OF US at one time or another have had to try to explain cricket to a foreigner – and what an impossible task it is, as Denzil Batchelor once found when he took a German to watch a match at Lord's. . . .

Denzil Batchelor:

My guest at a cricket match was a German, as thorough a representative of his country as Count Zeppelin, but with considerably smaller whiskers and more charm. The match we had under surveillance was Middlesex *v* Hampshire. My German friend stood by the doorway of the Long Room and wanted to shake hands with all those going on to the field of play. 'To wish a fair field and no favour,' he explained. I promised him that this was the way it would be. He then silently watched the play through enormous binoculars, through which (he explained) he had been able to see women and children running for shelter during daylight raids in the old days: 'The bad old days,' he added politely, bowing to the women and children in the Warner Stand.

At last he broke silence. 'The player Moss takes a very long run to the wicket. The player Titmus takes only a very short run. This is unfair to Titmus. He should be allowed a long one also.'

'He is. But he doesn't want one. His sort of bowling comes off better with a short run.'

'Moss is running twice as far as Titmus. Titmus should be allowed two balls for every ball Moss bowls, *nicht wahr*?'

Suddenly a bowler hit one of the Hampshire batsmen on the pad. 'I am of opinion that that is LBW,' exclaimed my guest, who with Germanic thoroughness had stayed up most of the night before, steeping himself in the laws. Dead silence – no one appealed.

'Could it not have been leg before wicket?'

'Quite possibly. I don't know. We shall never know. No one appealed.'

'But suppose it was leg before wicket, he is out?'

'Only if someone appeals.'

'But either he is *out* or he is *not out*. Appealing has nothing to do with it. Suppose the Middlesex team are all deaf mutes – what then? It is the duty of the umpire to see fair play. If a batsman who is out is allowed to continue his innings, is that fair play? I ask you – is that British?'

I replied that it was. Moss then bowled Horton, who departed for the pavilion.

'How so? Nobody asked whether he is out or not – yet he

goes. Was he any more out than the man who was leg before wicket?'

I found myself hoping that everyone would appeal for every possible question whether it was a catch at the wicket or a run out.

Towards the end of the day it began to get dark.

'If it gets too dark, who decides to stop the cricketing?'

'The umpires.'

'Where are their light-meters?'

'They don't have any. They just decide by their eyesight.'

'But light-meters have been invented. They are accurate and can be checked. The verdict of someone's eyesight is a mere matter of opinion.'

He shook his head, a man unconvinced that human instincts can ever be as good as a machine.

He tried another tack. 'Test matches are the greatest games you have,' he said. 'Why are they called that? What are they tests of?' I was too busy lighting a cigarette to answer.

'When you have Tests in England with Australia,' he asked, 'where do the umpires come from? India? The West Indies? South Africa?'

'They're English.'

'How is that possible? When an English team plays Rumania at football the referee is French. And even then there is almost a battle.'

Some dead-bat play had, fortunately, caught his interest' and he forgot about the umpires. 'How wide can a bat be?,

I told him.

He said: 'But a tennis racket can be any size: why not a cricket bat? I have often wondered whether it would be fair if, when a man wanted to win the last point of a close tennis match, he took up a racket as wide as the court and twenty feet high – and went to the net and just held it there.'

'You would have to ask the experts who made the original laws of lawn tennis.'

'Who were they?'

'The Marylebone Cricket Club.'

He did not look any the less puzzled.

'Could a lifelong member of the Labour Party umpire when Dexter is playing?'

'Yes, of course.'

'Could a Communist?'

'I don't know that Communists are very much interested in cricket.'

He studied the game through his binoculars intently, as if to prove beyond a shadow of a doubt that his political allegiance was unquestionable. At last he said with a sigh: 'Would you rather umpires had light-meters that gave perfect answers?'

I considered. 'No.'

'Would you rather have a sensible law that it was an umpire's duty to give a man out if he was out, whether anyone had appealed or not?'

This time I hardly had to think. 'No.'

'Are all cricket-lovers of your mind?'

'Yes, I expect so.'

He put his binoculars back in their case, as it was hardly worth bothering with them ever again.

'Come,' I said. 'Let us have a drink. What will you have?'

He said: 'Whisky is the smart drink of all Europe. Whisky, please.'

'What will you have with it?'

'Whisky.'

I sighed and gave the order.

* * *

Newly married young wife to her cricketer husband at the start of the second innings:

Let's go, John. This is where we came in.

* * *

An explanation of the game of cricket given to an American onlooker at Lord's:

It's quite simple. You have two sides, one out in the field, one in. Each man on the side that's in goes out, and when he's out he comes in, and the next man goes in until he's out. When they are all out the side that's out in the field comes in, and the side that's been in goes out and tries to get out those coming in. Sometimes you get men still in and not out. Then when both sides have been in and out, including 'not outs' that's the end of the game. Now do you see?'

* * *

Cricket from a feminine point of view:

I am engaged to a cricketer, and I have the feeling that my liking for the game was definitely the turning point in our relationship!

When my newly acquired boy-friend tentatively suggested that I should accompany him to a match I immediately imagined a baking hot summer's day spent reclining gracefully in a deckchair under a sunshade. If I chose to open my eyes I would see a small picturesque village green; if I chose to listen I would hear a subdued murmur of voices, and the gentle click of bat on ball. Peacefully I would acquire an even sun-tan until it was time for a delicious tea. . . .

My first match was in pouring rain on a muddy recreation ground which had been used for rugger in the winter. I was the only lady present, and tea was collected from a wooden hut; it consisted of scones – soggy as if penetrated by the prevailing drizzle – covered with a microscopic amount of butter followed by dry sponge. Hardly an auspicious beginning! Fortunately I was to find that my first taste of cricket was the exception, not the rule.

But in spite of this and other minor disadvantages, a surprisingly large number of women still continue to support the game. Ladies at cricket matches tend to unite – an isolated band in a masculine domain. One lady sat by me at her first cricket match, knitting busily, and also watching her beloved stride out to bat in the usual, unhurried fashion, as if the last thing he was interested in doing was batting. He bent to play his first ball. At this moment she dropped a stitch and when she looked up it was to see her crestfallen escort striding manfully back again, out that same first ball. Not realising the position, she smiled brightly and shouted: 'Darling, have you left your sweater behind?' He was teased about this for weeks.

Perhaps you find it difficult to understand why we women put up with the game? The answer is simple. We know when we're beaten! If I asked a confirmed cricketer to choose between me and cricket – well, I'll just say that I'm wise enough not to!

Seriously, I'm glad my fiancé loves cricket. It is a good thing to be able to share your beloved's interest, and it doesn't take him away from you – you can go with him! I may not yet know the difference between an off-break and a googly, but I'm learning, and probably the nicest thing about cricket is the cricketers themselves. For they are the friendliest, kindest bunch of men any woman could hope to find herself in the middle of, and, come to think of it, perhaps that's why we women still continue to support the game!

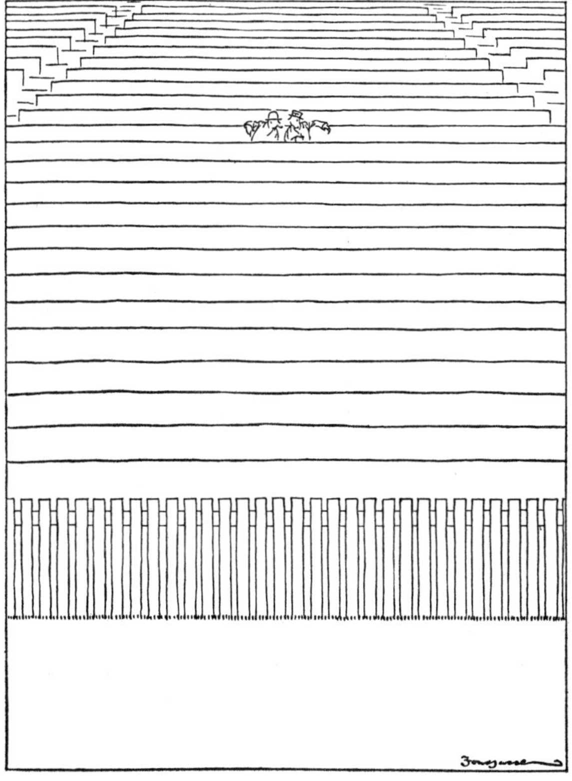

Of course, there's one thing that no foreigner will ever understand, and that's our enthusiasm for cricket.

Writers

AS I HAVE said in my introduction, more has been written about cricket than about all other games put together. Even without fiction there are hundreds of examples of wit in countless articles and books. I have therefore chosen some sample pieces from the works of half a dozen writers who, in my opinion, are the wittiest and best and who have also given me the most pleasure.

Advice to Cricket Writers:

Think before you Ink!

* * *

R C Robertson-Glasgow ('Cricket Prints') *about Philip Mead:*

He emerged from the pavilion with a strong, rolling gait; like a longshoreman with a purpose. He pervaded a cricket pitch. He occupied it and encamped on it. He erected a tent with a system of infallible pegging, then posted inexorable sentries. He took guard with the air of a guest who, having been offered a weekend by his host, obstinately decides to reside for six months. Having settled his whereabouts with the umpire, he wiggled the toe of his left boot for some fifteen seconds inside the crease, pulled the peak of a cap that seemed all peak, wiggled again, pulled again, then gave a comprehensive stare around him as if to satisfy himself that no fielder, aware of the task ahead, had brought out a stick of dynamite. Then he leaned forward and looked at you down the pitch, quite still. His bat looked almost laughingly broad.

* * *

From '46 Not Out' *by R C Robertson-Glasgow, describing a match in 1922 when he was playing for Oxford University:*

... One incident of rich humour relieved the dismal scene. It was against Surrey at the Oval. Tom Raikes and I were batting, at numbers ten and nine respectively. Tom was a Freshman from Winchester, a robust and clever bowler, with a be-damned-to-it attitude to life. It began by my playing a ball to the deep field at the Pavilion end. We ran our one comfortably, and when Tom asked if there was another, I said 'Yes' and we started for the second. Strange things then happened. As we were about to cross over, Tom suddenly turned round and scuttled back to his wicket. I followed him, but thinking this crease over-crowded I set out for the other (at the Pavilion end). Not to be outdone, Tom did the same. I beat him to it by a head. Meanwhile, the fielders, driven temporarily insane by these goings-on, were having a private game of rounders. At length the ball reached Strudwick, the wicketkeeper, who took off the bails. It was one thing to remove the bails, another to know who was out. We had occupied both ends two or three times each. The umpires, Bill Reeves and Frank Chester, stood impotent with laughter and doubt. But Tom solved the problem by striding away to the Pavilion. 'Over' was then called and as I prepared to receive the next ball, Bill Hitch, the Surrey fast bowler, said hoarsely at short-leg, 'You know who was out *really*, don't you?' But I didn't. Nor did he.

* * *

On 'Missing Catches' from 'Rain Stopped Play' *by R C Robertson-Glasgow:*

The easiest catch I ever saw was one missed by a Member of Parliament at mid-on. The ball, feebly struck, seemed scarcely equal, even with a gentle following breeze, to its brief journey; but the culprit, lost in the profundity of political cogitations, and further handicapped by tight trousers, lifted his head just in time to keep it lifted, and the ball, untouched by delaying finger, fell to the grass with an almost imperceptible and half-apologetic sound. Silence followed. The crime was beyond expiation. We could only stand helpless, as when a parishioner is seized by stomach-rumbles in the sermon or a host uses a bad word at a children's party.

There is usually a reason for a missed catch. For instance, when G O Allen, the England captain in the West Indies, floored a sitter at short-leg, he was doubtless exercised by anxiety as to what malady, and where, would lay low which of his fellow-fielders, and whether, to fill the widening breaches, any more cricketers could be persuaded to leave the shores of England. And, where there is no reason, there is apt to be a pretext; especially among the slips who, in moments of failure, excuse themselves by saying that the bowler bowled before they were ready; a condition that prevailed in a well-remembered match in a London suburb when my second slip, while watching his wife trying to park a car, took a snick on the back of the neck.

But the truly experienced misser is, paradoxically, the most alert. His rapidity of judgment is such that he can make any catch appear impossible. If in the slips, he hurls himself sideways or forwards, clawing the air with all the desperation of a drowning man, and so invests a bad miss with the romance of a near-miracle. If situated in the deeper positions, he realises, as soon as the catch goes up, that if he stands quite still the ball cannot miss him. He must therefore decide which course will win him most sympathy among the dupes, to run forward and let the ball pass high over his head, or to totter backwards and watch it drop in front of him, or, easier yet, to take a few graceful steps to the side and shield his eyes from the sun.

But perhaps the simplest method of all is to fall down. To those who favour this idea my advice is, once down, stay down. The effect is blunted by any attempt to rise; and I recall, with pleasure, the ironical applause which greeted a Somerset deep-fielder who fell while misjudging a towering hit by Percy Chapman, then half-rose into an attitude of oriental devotion.

The lot of the bowler is indeed unenviable. Besides the perfection of pitches and the indifference of umpires he must suffer day in and out from fielders who conjoin to natural incompetence every art of hypocrisy.

*　*　*

From 'Talking of Cricket' *by Ian Peebles:*

. . . The health of the side, although jealously guarded, at times gave much cause for anxiety. Later on when we arrived at the fateful field of Thunderpore, strains and dysentry, in varying degrees of severity, had robbed us of half our numbers, and we were hard pressed to raise eleven mobile, if not able, bodies. But the die being cast, that is having lost the toss again, we tottered into the arena, and the match got under way.

The first few overs delivered by Alf Gover, then recently risen from a bed of sickness, were uneventful. During the third, only the most acute observer would have been alarmed at the tense expression on his face as he started on his long, hustling run. It was when he shot past the crouching umpire and thundered down the pitch with the undelivered ball in his hand that it became obvious that something was amiss. The batsman, fearing a personal assault, sprang smartly backward, but the flannelled giant sped past looking neither to right nor left. Past wicketkeeper, slips and fine leg in a flash, he hurtled up the pavilion steps in a cloud of dusty gravel and was gone. That he has never received full credit for this record is due to the lack of timing apparatus and the distance, from the start of his run to his uncomfortable destination, not being a recognised one.

As, in the tight-lipped precipitation of his flight, he had been unable to give any hint of his future movements, fine leg, after a moment's thought, followed up the steps and, having rescued the ball from the bowler's convulsive grasp, announced that we had better start looking for a substitute.

*　*　*

'The Umpire' from 'The Good Days' by Neville Cardus*:*

Cricket has begun; the umpires have walked to the wicket, and they have adjusted the stumps with the precision of great masters of geometry. Probably they have bowled a ball up and down the pitch to one another, just to let the crowd understand that they too have in their time been mighty hunters before the Lord. And the cry of 'Play!' has been uttered decisively and authoritatively.

The umpire is the law of cricket personified, image of the noble constitution of the best of games. He can make or mar the match for us. A bad umpire means bad-tempered cricketers, and, therefore, bad play. Yet how little notice we take of the umpire, once we have seen him step into his onerous office. It is only when he commits a blunder that we realise he is there. Often is the phrase 'A bad decision' heard amongst cricketers, but how seldom any of us talk about and praise a good decision!

The umpire at cricket is like the geyser in the bathroom; we cannot do without it, yet we notice it only when it is out of order. The solemn truth is that the umpire is the most important man on the field; he is like the conductor of an orchestra. If first slip misses a catch, the error involves only a personal fallibility; we say 'Hard luck!' and first slip begins again. If the umpire falters, everybody in the game is drawn into the range of mortal frailty; we do not say 'Hard luck!' to the miserable man in the white coat; we even add to our

THE MONOLOGUE

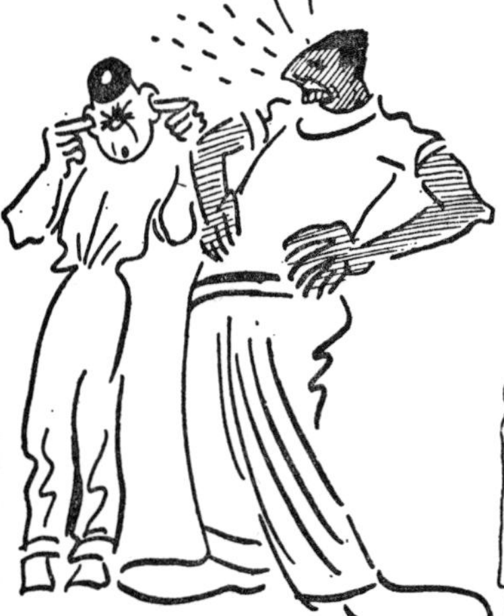

AND MR TATE IS SUCH AN INCESSANT CHATTERER ON THE FIELD THAT —

RATTLE
RATTLE
RATTLE

EVEN THE UMPIRES HAVE GREAT DIFFICULTY IN ACHIEVING THEIR 140 WINKS

MR TATE LIKES CONVERSATION SO MUCH THAT WHEN THEY PUT HIM IN THE FIELD OUT OF EAR-SHOT HE TALKS TO HIMSELF EVEN IF HE DOESN'T KNOW THE ANSWERS.

LEAVING MR TATE AND HIS ELOQUENCE FOR THE MOMENT WE SHOULD LIKE TO POINT OUT THAT AFTER A SPLENDID TEA INTERVAL THE UMPIRES CAME OUT AND IN FULL VIEW OF EVERYBODY HAD A GOOD LIE DOWN

Tom Webster 32

gloating over his fallibility the imputation of stupidity or of malice prepense. If the batsman misses a half-volley and is bowled, the crowd laughs or, at the worst, calls the guilty one an ass. But the umpire who errs as obviously as that is likely to be regarded as unfit for his job. His fallibility can be reported at Lord's; nobody reports to Lord's the cricketer who in the excitement of the moment runs his partner out.

All day long, ball after ball, the umpire must keep his mind intensely on the game. The players are free to enjoy relaxations. Some of them indulge in a good sleep while their side is batting. When rain falls and stops play, the cricketers can forget the match for a while. The umpire enjoys no release from responsibility; until the match is over, or until weather causes an abandonment, he is obliged to watch, watch, watch – either the play or the pitch or the groundsman.

The amount of concentration he is expected to perform every day is almost an abuse of human endurance. What a great country this would be if every man, whatever his station, concentrated half as much on the smallest detail of his work as an umpire is compelled to do, from high noon to dewy evening of a cricket match!

The umpires are the Dogberries of the game. We see them as essentially comic characters. Whenever a batsman swipes to leg, and hits the umpire in the small of the back, how the crowd roars! If the wind blows the hat off the umpire's head, laughter holds sides. The reason for the humour which comes out of the activities of the umpires is a matter of deep psychology. For the simple fact is that no man can sustain with dignity the semblance of infallible judgment. Man is born to sin and error; and when he wears the robes of virtue and wisdom and law and infallibility all rolled into one, the gods infect us with their merriment.

'How's that?' shrieked the whole field when a batsman was brilliantly thrown out. 'Wait a minute,' answered the umpire. 'Who did it?'

It is, of course, to country cricket that we must look for the really comical Dogberry of the crease. I remember Old George, in the days when we used to go on a jolly tour through Shropshire. The custom was for each side to bring its own umpire, and at the beginning of every match old George made a point of meeting the other team's umpire over a glass of ale in the pavilion.

'Now, look 'ee 'ere,' he would say, 'it is for yew to luke after yewre business, and Oi'll luke after mine!'

Once on a time a cricket match was about to be played between two village clubs of long and vehement rivalry. An hour before the pitching of stumps a visitor to the district walked on to the ground and inspected the wicket. He was greeted by an old man, a very old man. The visitor asked for information about the impending battle, and the ancient monument told him.

'Is your team strong in bowling?' asked the visitor.

'Ay, sir, not so bad,' was the answer.

'And who gets most of your wickets?' asked the visitor.

'Why, sir, Oi do,' was the reply.

'Heavens,' said the visitor, 'surely you don't bowl at your time of life?'

'No, sir, Oi be the umpire.'

But in the highest realms of county and Test cricket the umpire, though frequently the source of humour, is seldom allowed to share in it. A crucial blunder might mean an end to his livelihood. He deserves all the help he can possibly be given. Is not his job difficult enough in itself without the addition of embarrassments which are the consequence of our hastiness and temper? I appeal to every lover of the game to think of the umpire always, to bear always in mind that, like the backwoods pianist, he is doing his best – in threatening circumstances.

English cricket today is fortunate to be under the supervision of umpires as fine and courageous and clever as Arthur Morton (a rich character), Frank Chester, Hardstaff – to name but a few. Chester is a joy to watch; he delivers his decisions sometimes with immense irony. I have seen him signal a snicked boundary by means of a gesture of regal disdain, as though to say, 'What a stroke! I am compelled by the law to rule it worth four; but I reserve the right to say what I think about it.'

I have seen Chester give a batsman out with a finger suddenly pointed to heaven, dramatic in its announcement of ruthless finality. And I have seen him turn his back on a bowler's manifestly absurd appeal for leg-before-wicket –

turn his back with the air of a man consigning another to some place outside the pale of all sense and decency.

Arthur Morton is not so spectacular; he believes in the conservation of energy. But county cricketers know well, and revel in, his comments at the wicket, many of them delivered out of the corner of the mouth. 'I wish you'd keep quiet,' he once said at the agony of a Lancashire and Yorkshire match; 'it's like umpiring in a parrot-house.'

Parry is the umpire who bends himself into a right angle for every ball when he is standing at the bowler's end; he takes on this terrible burden of physical discomfort so that, as he thinks, he can get a better sight of the ball in a leg-before-wicket mix-up. Merely to look at him for an hour is to go home suffering from lumbago. They all of them are worthy of our applause, the men who serve the game by standing – and waiting for the end of the long, long day.

* * *

From 'The Art of Coarse Cricket' *by Spike Hughes:*

UMPIRING AND INTERPRETATION OF THE LAWS. Even if you arrive at the scene of the match with only five players it is essential that you should always arrive with your own umpire. A good umpire must be above all suspicion, but having shown that he is he must not be above exploiting his reputation in favour of your side. In other words, he must make the most of the fact that to err is human, at the same time disguising this failing so carefully that his more biased judgments appear divine in their impartiality and wisdom.

One of the first things demanded of your umpire is that he should be helpful, especially when your side is fielding. He should not wait for an appeal from the bowler for LBW nor from the wicket-keeper for a catch at the wicket. He should raise his finger as soon as he sees the ball hit the pad or hears the sound of a snick and draw the bowler's attention to the incident with a startled whistle or an audibly astonished 'Cor!' The bowler can then ask 'How's that?' and receive a favourable verbal confirmation. This method of umpiral guidance was practised for many years by the local umpire of a Sussex village where I used to play. Bert could never have been accused of flagrantly biased judgment; it was just that if he sensed any doubt in the bowler's or wicket-keeper's mind and they were at all hesitant in appealing he made up their minds for them. Bert not only wanted to see his village make the most of every possible chance; he was also the local cobbler and depended for a large part of his livelihood on fixing spikes into our boots properly. Business to Bert, after all, was Business, say what you like.

In contrast to Bert, of Sussex, you occasionally encounter the umpire whose honesty and impartiality of judgment are most perversely unhelpful. My friend Edgar, who travelled for many seasons as our regular umpire when he had tired of being caught at cover every time he made the off-drive he had learned at Harrow, was always scrupulously fair so long as it didn't really matter. Such an excellent umpire both on and off the field, indeed, that in order that he should not be asked to forgo his racing on Saturdays we played all our fixtures on Sundays (he also had a car). But Edgar's eccentricity we discovered – only after nearly a season of matches – was an extreme choosiness as to who made the appeal. It was no good raising a communally deafening shout of 'How's that?' for a catch at the wicket if the bowler himself didn't appeal.

Playing once against the village where the racing stables are (it was Edgar who originally arranged this fixture), I was bowling downwind with Edgar standing at my end. A palpable catch was taken at the wicket; there was a roar. from players and spectators alike.

Edgar, grinding his shooting stick more firmly into the ground, gave the batsman not out.

'What do you mean?' I asked, ' "Not Out"?' (Coarse Cricket being a democratic pastime the parry and thrust of debate and general discussion of matters of public interest are part of the fabric of our Way of Life.)

'You didn't appeal.'

'I know. It was barely necessary. It was so obvious.'

'Why didn't you appeal?'

'I told you. Anyway, I didn't hear it.' (I am rather deaf in one ear.)

'You should have appealed.'

'Did you hear it?'

'No. It's downwind.' (Edgar is rather deaf in one ear, too.) 'But I saw it.'

'But the wicket-keeper heard it – and caught it.'

'I know. But that's not enough. The bowler's got to appeal.'

'All right. "How's that?" '.

'Too late now. I've already said "not out".'

'Oh. But he was out, wasn't he?'

'Yes, of course. Everybody knows that.'

The meeting then passed on to other business.

Standing, or rather sitting, on his shooting-stick, at square-leg, Edgar was just as methodical in his umpiring as he was at the bowler's end. But in this position, perhaps, his interpretation of the Laws, if not so personal, gave greater satisfaction to us when we were in the field. Edgar went on the theory that if he made a slight error of judgment in our favour it was almost impossible to prove it. Thus a doubtful appeal for stumping would always be allowed, provided the bails were whipped off tidily and the appeal convincing, on the the grounds that the batsman had lifted his heel off the ground for a fleeting and no longer re-capturable second. Similarly, in the excitement that accompanies an attempted running out, Edgar could always justify his decision in our favour by pointing out that the batsman had neglected to ground his bat as he ran to the crease. The evidence of the photo-finish has not yet been accepted in Coarse Cricket, and if you ask me it is just as well. There is no need for it, anyway, so long as everybody understands that the Umpire's Decision is Final.

The principle guiding that final decision is one that covers all eventualities: 'If, in the opinion of the Umpire . . .' Thus we have no haggling over the MCC's latest LBW rule; we have no time for calculating any Euclidean proposition concerning the ball pitching in a line described etc. If, in the opinion of the Umpire, the ball would have hit the wicket then the batsman is out and that is all there is to it. This, of course, applies only to your bowlers. When your side is batting, the MCC rule is applied literally and your umpire's reason for giving the batsman not out is far too complicated and abstruse to explain without a set square and a book of log tables, so that – once more – the Umpire's Decision must be accepted as Final. And if this axiom is questioned then doubts are raised at once and the batsman is, of course, to be given the benefit of them.

Circumstances are held to alter cases, and the Coarse Cricket umpire who does not recognise that this applies more to your side than to your opponent's is best left behind. Even if he has got a car.

Getting home:

The purpose of drawing stumps at 6.55 pm on any Sunday match has already been hinted at in an earlier section.

It was not pointed out, however, that to make absolutely certain there is no further play after this, those batsmen on your side who have had their innings should be encouraged to change into civilian dress as soon as they return to the pavilion. In most cases they will need no prompting in this, for even if the match be finished with an hour or more to spare, no true Coarse Cricketer either expects or is prepared for a serious second innings after the result of the match has been decided.

To pass the time, on the other hand, there are several variants of what is known as The Beer Match to be played although, in passing, it is sad to note that in recent years there has been an increasing tendency to forget that it is meant to be a Beer Match and that the losers are expected to stand pints all round to the victors. Nevertheless, it must be admitted that the playing of the match can be almost as worthwhile as the prize for which it is played.

One popular form of the Beer Match is to have each side bat for thirty minutes. This speeds up the rate of play beyond all recognition and we have the welcome spectacle of the incoming batsmen running towards the wicket to save time. The variant which I personally prefer, however, is that in which everybody on the side, including the player who deposes the regular wicket-keeper, bowls one over each. This not only reveals some unexpected bowling talent, but frequently also the effectiveness of lobs, sneakers and balls bowled by the wicket-keeper which, if they ever pitched on the ground, would be devasting leg-breaks. Or so he says.

At 6.55 pm it would appear that the Organiser-Captain's day's work is done, for there remain for him only to collect the empty beer jugs and glasses together to return to the pub, recover his score book, return all borrowed equipment to the opposition's dressing-room and round up the odd shoes, cricket boots and socks his own side have left behind in their rush to leave the ground. On reaching the pub himself, however, the Captain becomes a full-time Organiser again for the rest of the evening. He will find that half the people that owe him money for tea have slunk away early, while those who remain complicate things almost unendurably by never having any change or, indeed, any visible means of support apart from a ready supply of promissory notes.

With the landlord's bill for food and drink and glasses broken in the dressing-room finally (thanks to your remembering to bring your cheque book) paid off, the Organiser – if he is lucky – may be able to settle down to a period of carefree social intercourse and post mortem discussion of the day's events. But it will not be for long, for as the evening draws on and closing time looms only an hour ahead there will be a general proposal that all should repair to that pub along the road everybody stopped at on the way down. Whether the proposal is accepted or not, in any case the whole question of Transport rears its ugly head once more. Passengers who came down in one car in the morning are now without transport because that particular driver has had to leave early. But after many assertions that you'll take Michael if somebody else will squeeze in David, Tony and that Old Harrovian whose name you still haven't discovered, you will find that, in the end, it is easier to get your players from the fixture than it was to get them to it twelve hours previously.

After closing time, on the final stage of the journey back to town, the Organiser may hope to relax. He has got his team to the ground, on and off the field, and finally launched them on their way home. It will have cost him a pretty packet but he will reflect that it was worth it; and if David, who is now in the same car with him, is complaining that he has left his shoes in The Greyhound at Chalfont St Peter and will have to make his way through London in his socks, then at least it is no longer the Organiser's responsibility. In any case, David can pick up his shoes on the way to Great Missenden next year.

In his capacity as Captain the Organiser may reflect too that he has executed his duties satisfactorily, nursed his team to victory or an honourable defeat and afterwards exercised tact and diplomacy in making small-talk with the players' wives who showed an understandable but regrettable inclination to want to go home far too early. The Coarse Cricket Captain's work, like a woman's, is never done, and when – long after midnight – he finally gets to sleep, he does so with the full knowledge that in addition to the whole business starting up all over again the next morning he will be so stiff from bowling too long that he can hardly move to the telephone to start collecting his team for the next fixture a fortnight hence.

Perhaps there are easier ways of playing cricket; I do not know. But there are few pastimes at once so rewarding, so entertaining and stimulating for all the attendant anxieties, disappointments and expense as a good game of Coarse Cricket.

* * *

Strange as it may seem there are *people who don't enjoy playing cricket and I'm afraid that when forced to do so at school, they go through a very miserable time – as Arthur Marshall once explained in a talk for the BBC entitled 'Playing the Game':*

I was not gifted at cricket. For nine years I was a youthful sacrificial victim on the altar of our dreaded national game. I was not alone. Hundreds of thousands of young persons suffered with me, and suffer still. I estimate that nearly two thousand hours or about eighty-four days or twelve whole weeks of one's life were spent in beflannelled misery in the middle of a green field, longing to be elsewhere. No, luckily enough not always right in the middle. Having proved myself a duffer at anything requiring speedy action near the bat and wickets, I spent a comparatively happy two years in a position well known at prep schools but without any official recognition. I refer to the vital post of Long Stop. It is to be found immediately behind the wicket-keeper on the very boundary of the field of play and it has a great deal to recommend it.

Its chief charm lay in the fact that there was only one chance in five of you ever being drawn into the picture. The ball when bowled might hit the batsman, the batsman might hit it, it might hit the wicket, it might hit the wicket-keeper. When it missed all these hazards and came towards you, you found yourself in the very thick of it. All, however, was not lost. The grass in the outfield tended to be long and lush and if it had not recently been mown there was a good chance of the ball stopping before it ever got to you. No point in meeting trouble half-way. Ignoring unmannerly shouts to run, you waited for the ball to come to rest and then, leaping smartly forward, you picked it up and threw it briskly in, thus skilfully preventing the batsmen from crossing for the fourth time.

At school we faced the tyranny of cricket, and of all games, in the same uncomplaining way that we faced surds, fractions, Canada's exports, Euclid, Africa's imports and the Hundred Years War. It was all part of the scholastic merry-go-round. Daily we put on those hot and unsuitable clothes, the bags supported by a school belt with snake clasp, and on our heads we placed those enormous, shapeless, white flannel bonnets without which small boys were thought to succumb instantly from sunstroke. Beneath a tree was the visible scoring apparatus, a selection of white numbers on sheets of black tin hung on a discarded blackboard and mysteriously known as the tallywag. The boys who worked this were a sort of walking wounded, boys recovering from boils or headaches or lunch or asthmatic attacks and they had behind them a long tradition of indolence and lack of co-operation. They lay on their stomachs chewing nougat and reading another chapter of *Tarzan of the Apes* or *Bulldog Drummond*. When they tired of that, they would just aimlessly hit each other for five minutes or so. From time to time a despairing cry would reach them from the pitch – 'TALLYWAG' – and they would then reluctantly change the tin plates to a score that was possibly accurate to the nearest ten. At the end of play they were allowed their little joke, which was to leave the blackboard showing that the final score had been 999 for ONE, the last player making 998.

For matches against other schools, the school pavilion was much in evidence. Its interior smelt strongly of disinfectant and linseed-oil and for its construction reliance had been largely placed on corrugated iron. Within could be found cricket nets and spiders and grubby pads and spiders and old team photographs and old spiders. There was also a bat signed by Hobbs which was proudly displayed to the opposing players in a spirit of unconscious Gamesmanship. But despite this trophy, a sad air of failure and decay pervaded the building. From its window, innumerable cricketing disasters had been witnessed; for example, our defeat by Dumbleton Park when our total score had been eight, three of which were byes. There had been, too, the shaming day when our captain, out first ball, had burst into a torrent of hysterical tears.

But cricket did have one supreme advantage over football.

It could be stopped by rain. Every morning at prayers, devout non-cricket-lovers put up a plea for a downpour. Being in England, our prayers were quite frequently answered!

Must have been big fellahs . . . just see where the leg stump's gone.

Short of a Length

REAL WIT frequently loses itself in the recital of drawn-out stories, when an audience becomes impatient and out of humour when the climax does arrive. The following snippets illustrate the advantage of 'keeping it short':

A cricket enthusiast kept three trays on the desk in his office marked IN, OUT, and LBW. When asked what the LBW stood for he replied: 'Let the Blighters Wait.'

* * *

A very bad wicket-keeper was nicknamed the Ancient Mariner by his team mates because 'He stoppeth one of three.'

* * *

A keen Nottinghamshire supporter in the thirties called his dachshund Larwood – because it had four short legs.

* * *

A somewhat rude sports columnist once described MCC as 'The only lunatic asylum in Great Britain which is run by the inmates.'

* * *

'Modern cricket's like modern beer, I reckon. A little less o' science and a little more o' nature ud do 'em both a power o' good.'

* * *

A club cricketer received a printed circular from the secretary informing him and other members that the club subscription was going up by one pound per *anum*. He replied by return that he preferred to continue paying through the *nose*!

* * *

The Late Lord Knutsford:

God could have produced a better berry than a strawberry but He never did, and He could have put it into the mind of man to invent a better game than cricket but He never did.

* * *

Unknown batsman on being asked on his return to the pavilion what he had thought of a certain fast bowler's bowling:

Don't know – I only heard it.

*   *   *

An extract from a newspaper report:

And then with his score at 137 he was clean bowled by a ball which he ought to have left alone.

*   *   *

William Douglas-Home was never a very good cricketer and when at Eton played in a fairly low-standard game. One day he read in the Eton College 'Chronicle' *that the captain of the XI had not made many runs recently as he had struck a bad patch. He commented:*

He should come and play on some of the pitches which we have to use, and he would strike a few more.

*   *   *

A Melbourne lady who knew her cricket was discussing Lord Harris with a friend during the Tour of Australia in 1878:

I hear Lord Harris is a good catch.

Her companion, who did not know her cricket:

Not at all, dear – the man's married.

* * *

A certain bishop speaking about the funeral of the Hon F S Jackson:

. . . There were hundreds of cricketers at the service and as I looked down on the rapt faces of the vast congregation I could see how their hearts went out to the great man and how they revered him as though he were the Almighty, only infinitely stronger on the leg-side.

* * *

During a BBC programme which was touring European capitals, the panel was asked by a Dutchman in Amsterdam, 'Why don't you bet on cricket in England?':

Lady Bonham-Carter replied: 'Oh, in England, cricket is a religion and you don't bet on God, do you?'

* * *

By a Worcester member between the wars after a dull innings by Bull, followed by an even slower one by Buller:

Well we've had Bull and Buller. Thank goodness there isn't a Bullest playing for us!

* * *

Charles Bray in the 'Daily Herald' *after Denis Compton's injury in the 1948 Test v Australia at Old Trafford:*

. . . Compton saved England's face at the expense of his own. . . .

* * *

During one of the usual Saturday afternoon round-ups of cricket on Sports Service, the BBC commentator at Edgbaston apologised for handing over late to the commentator at Leyton, Essex:

Better Leyton than never.

* * *

When George Mann, captain of MCC, was dismissed by the late 'Tufty' Mann, the South African slow left arm bowler, during the 1948–49 tour of South Africa, John Arlott commented over the radio:

Mann's inhumanity to Mann.

* * *

Stephen Potter describing a celebrated gamesman:

He was the first to enclose the complete records of cricket in the cover of Bradshaw's Railway Guide, so that when, in order to win an argument, he was 'recalling' say, Verity's bowling average of 1931 he was able to achieve accuracy up to two places of decimals, while to the admiring onlookers it seemed that he was casually verifying the time of a train.

* * *

A new batsman, who looked particularly pleased with himself, walked down the pavilion steps and made his way slowly out to the pitch. On arrival he asked for guard and then carefully took off one of the bails to make a mark from the popping crease to the stumps. He then looked round the field in a professional way and called for the sightscreen to be moved a couple of feet. He asked for a fresh guard, fiddled with his cap, twiddled his bat round in his hand, and prepared to meet his first ball. It clean bowled him, spreadeagling the stumps in all directions. As he made his way back to the pavilion he passed the third man who said to him:

Bad luck sir, just as you were getting set. . . .

* * *

SPORTING OLD PARSON: Why is a ball like that called a Yorker, sir?

PROFESSIONAL PLAYER: A Yorker, sir? Oh, when the ball's pitched right up to the block. . . .

SPORTING OLD PARSON: Yes, yes – I didn't ask you what a Yorker was – (with dignity) – I know that as well as you do. But *why* is it called a Yorker?

PROFESSIONAL PLAYER: Well, I can't say, sir? I don't know what else you *could* call it.

* * *

Cardew Robinson in a poem entitled 'The Honest Batsman'*:*

No, I didn't lift my head a simple fraction,
My left elbow – it was well and truly bent.
Yes, I played right down the line,
And the ball had lost its shine,
So it didn't swerve to any great extent.
No, the wicket isn't green, nor is it sticky,
It's as true as any wicket well could be;
Yes, conditions are so nice,
They're a batsman's paradise,
But a paradise soon lost alas – for me.
No, the ball was not a bouncer nor a bumper
No, it didn't turn an inch from off to leg,
No, it wasn't sheer bad luck,
That I'm back here for a duck,

So please spare me your condolences, I beg.
No, it wasn't a leg-cutter nor a yorker;
No, it didn't turn, or twist or sway or swing:
It just pleaded to be hit,
Why I'm out I must admit –
IS BECAUSE I WENT AND MISSED THE RUDDY
THING!

Would you mind taking middle-and leg? I'm on TV as well as you, you know.

Acknowledgements

I should like to express my thanks and acknowledge my indebtedness to the authors and publishers of the following:

Cricket Prints by the late R C Robertson-Glasgow (T Werner Laurie Ltd, reprinted by permission of A D Peters)
'Cricket Through Other Eyes' by Denzil Batchelor (*Playfair Cricket Monthly*)
46 NOT OUT by the late R C Robertson-Glasgow (Hollis and Carter)
Playing the Game by Arthur Marshall (BBC)
Punch Article by Bernard Hollowood (Punch Publications Ltd)
Rain Stopped Play by the late R C Robertson-Glasgow (Dennis Dobson Ltd)
Speech at the 1961 Forty Club Dinner by Humphrey Tilling
Talking of Cricket by Ian Peebles (Museum Press)
The Art of Coarse Cricket by Spike Hughes (Hutchinson)
The Good Days by Sir Neville Cardus (Rupert Hart-Davis Ltd)
The Honest Batsman by Cardew Robinson (Macdonald and Co Ltd.

'When Milady Fainted in the Soup' by J J Warr (*Sunday Telegraph*)
Cricket from a Feminine Point of View by Jenny Hill

I should also like to express my gratitude for permission to reproduce cartoons by the following:

The late Fougasse (Punch Publications Ltd)
Hargreaves (Hammond, Hammond)
Bernard Hollowood (Punch Publications Ltd)
David Langdon (Punch Publications Ltd)
Starke (Punch Publications Ltd)
Roy Ullyett (*Daily Express*)
Varney (Leslie Frewin Publishers)
The late Tom Webster (*Daily Mail*)